D0877185

TIM KLABUNDE

NET-WORK LIKE AN INTRO-VERT

A NEW WAY OF thinking about BUSINESS relationships.

Published by Asset Beam Publishing Ltd.

Copyright © 2012 Tim Klabunde

All rights reserved. No portion of this book may be reproduced, stored in a retrieval system, or transmitted in any form or by any means — electronic, mechanical, photocopy, recording, scanning, or other — except for brief quotations in critical reviews or articles, without the prior written permission of the author.

Details in some anecdotes and stories have been changed to protect the identities of the persons involved.

ISBN-13: 978-0981081670

DEDICATION

This book is dedicated to my dad, for the unending hours spent proofing my articles and blog posts over the years, continuing to guide me as I have struggled to better understand relationships, through it all teaching me about what really matters in life. I am truly blessed to have a father who never stopped being my dad. Thank you.

CONTENTS

PREFACE:
AN INTROVERT'S VIEW
OF NETWORKING

I am an introvert. As a marketer, I began trying to learn how to network effectively many years ago but was rapidly disheartened by what I found.

It seemed as if every networking expert that I heard speak or whose books I read an extreme extrovert. Instead of leveraging my strengths as an introvert, they were trying to teach me how to sell using *their* formulas for success. I learned how to give an "elevator pitch," that is, a sales pitch you can tell someone in about the time it takes to ride an elevator. I learned how to "work a room" to ensure that I would meet the five key people I was targeting. I even learned the fine art of how to ensure that someone would give me their business card for follow-up. While I got fairly good at this type of networking, somewhere inside I couldn't help but recognize that I wasn't being true to myself. I had taught myself to be someone else, and I simply did not enjoy networking.

So I started over.

I gave up the sales pitch, the techniques of how to effectively work a room, and decided to start from scratch. I searched out introverts who were successful at networking, and I learned from them. I read and wrote on real relationship development in an effort to better understand people. I tried new things and tested theories.

Over the course of several years, I developed a refreshing approach to networking that I now refer to as Real Networking. It was a great feeling that took over as I realized that I could, in fact, enjoy networking as an introvert! I had discovered something that would help me for the rest of my life, but what came next was a complete surprise.

In the fall of 2008, my network had grown to the point where I thought it would be fun to get everyone together after work just to, well, network. It might seem crazy that an introvert would ever consider getting a bunch of people together, but honestly it just felt natural, if not fun.

These were just my friends and we simply were going to meet up, talk business and life, and have a relaxing time. So, I sent out an invitation to several people in my network to get together at a restaurant in Arlington, Virginia. They, in turn, sent out open invitations to people they knew. We had a space reserved that could hold 75 people and I expected that 50 might show up, but what happened next astounded me.

It wasn't that a handful of people came. It wasn't that a lot of people came. It was that an amazing number of people showed up simply to connect after work! By the time the evening was over, I had counted 142 people at our little get-together.

Looking back on that first event, it is easy to recognize that they hadn't all come because of me or the person who had invited them. Rather, they had all come because they were also looking for something else…relationships. I had accidentally stumbled into Real Networking, and people from all over also seemed to be looking for it! So, I decided to see if it could be repeated.

Two months later, I found a larger venue and sent out word through my network again to spread news about the event, and this time I set up a way that people could RSVP. On April 29, 2009, the strength of our little introvert network was tested when I hosted a second networking event.

As an introvert, I've got to tell you that I never imagined that I would host a networking event with 20 people attending—much less more than a hundred—so I had complete confidence that if this was going to ever work, it could only be something else that was causing the success. What I never comprehended could happen was that 344 people would register to attend that second event in April.

Today, that same network has over 40,000 members, and we have hosted events in nine cities across the United States! It turns out I'm not the only person who is looking for more than sales pitches; I think that you might be one of those people also.

I hope that this book is the start of something new for you, just as the information in it was the start of something new for me. My goal is to show you how to change your approach to people, not solely for the purposes of networking and business, but also because these same principals can change your personal relationships.

If you are ready to make a change for the better, then get ready for an exciting journey that will yield the greatest friendships of your life.

Tim Klabunde

1

NETWORKING IS
NOT SELLING

I n May of 2005, I was finally fed up with networking. According to the "experts" I had done everything right. I had learned and implemented the "proper" networking techniques to be successful, but it never quite felt right. Every time I went to an event, I felt as if I had to act like someone else. The "proper" techniques I had learned didn't seem to get at the root of Real Networking.

I had always thought networking was about relationships, and I couldn't help but feel that much of what I was doing seemed to be centered on what I could get from other people, rather than developing a true, mutually beneficial relationship. I had to admit that I was having some success, but I was certain that there was a better way to network than to act like someone else. There had to be a way to network like an introvert.

It was about that time I met John. John wasn't one of the people who used all of the networking tips I had learned; rather, he was a friend. It was always refreshing to be around John. He had an amazing way of motivating me to do everything in my power to help him.

Like me, John was an introvert, so his approach was different from the one I had been taught. He provided me with leads, regularly sent me pertinent information on projects, and was always opening new doors for me by introducing me to other people. In short, he was always trying to help make me successful. Because John was working so hard for me, I wanted to work just as hard for him. As a result, the moment I would get a new lead I would send it to John, and I always found myself trying to reciprocate his unending help and friendship.

I found it interesting that I received more leads from John than from any person I met at networking events. Moreover, the quality of the relationships built with those he introduced me to were always far superior to any relationship that I made elsewhere.

John is one of those guys who can pick up the phone and bring more work in the door in one day than others do in a year. He has learned to succeed at networking, not by perfecting his elevator speech or collecting business cards, but through the knowledge that developing one strong relationship is better than developing a thousand acquaintances.

This is what made John such an amazing networker—he helped people all the time. He was proactive with a core group of individuals, and they were likewise always looking for ways to help him. His approach created numerous mutually beneficial relationships that could be characterized as a core group of people who were working together to help one another. It created a powerful network! I recognized that not only could John do this, but I, or anyone else for that matter, could also implement it. All I needed to do was to focus on helping others succeed! Finally, networking was beginning to make sense as I began focusing on what networking was always intended to be: building relationships.

For years, we have been told that extroverts are better networkers than introverts, and there is no doubt that would be true if networking was about getting more business cards than your competition.

But John taught me something valuable. He taught me that networking isn't about business cards; it's about building relationships. It is time we reevaluate how we network and learn a few lessons from introverts on networking.

An introvert's litmus test

I was amazed the day it all started to click. If relationships are the foundation of networking, then building relationships must be the objective. It was as if I suddenly had a litmus test through which I could evaluate all of the networking tools I had been taught.

The litmus test was simple: does this build a relationship? What truly shocked me was the astounding number of networking activities that I was doing that failed this litmus test. It was official. The so-called experts might be right for a limited number of extreme extroverts, but for the typical introvert, they were teaching a failed model.

So I started over.

I started redefining networking. As I tested tools and ideas against the relationship litmus test, a new trend started to emerge. I began to realize that, almost universally, **relationships grow when two people are working selflessly to help each another succeed.** I also noted that the inverse is true, that relationships suffer when actions are taken out of selfish motivation.

Have you ever had someone help you out to the degree that you sat at your desk and simply pondered what you could do to return the favor? One such situation happened for me several years ago when a friend helped to get me on a team for a major project that resulted in the largest federal contract my firm was ever awarded. What took her 15 minutes (time spent selling someone else on using my firm's services) would have cost me 40 hours of phone calls, multiple lunches, and numerous meetings. Even with this effort, I still wouldn't have been guaranteed a spot on the team. Needless to say, I was not only thankful to my friend for her work, but I literally sat at my desk working up ways to return the favor.

The key to this story isn't how she helped me to get on the team; it is how your actions can motivate other people to help you. Those 15 minutes of work have resulted in dozens of referrals and project leads for her, as I have worked to return the favor. As my friend focused on helping me, she was developing a mutually beneficial relationship that resulted in me working hard to help her.

Networking is helping other people

When you help someone, it creates an innate and positive response. If I were to refer you to a new client, you would probably be inwardly appreciative. You might even send me a quick thank-you email. If, over the next two weeks, I was to help you on three additional occasions, giving you valuable information, introducing you to a potential client, and referring a new project to you, you would probably take notice. You might start thinking of how you could help me in return, and, at a minimum, you would be grateful.

But here is the kicker. If, over the next two months, I was to help you more than twenty times, sending you leads, referrals, and information to help you succeed, you would develop a healthy desire to return the favor. Whether it's from a desire to keep the help coming or as an innate response, we know that most humans will have an urgent and positive desire to reciprocate help that is received.

Moreover, most people become excited about helping someone who has helped them, and they will look proactively for opportunities to reciprocate. Imagine if you were doing this type of networking with just ten people. As you helped each of them several times a week, they likewise were helping you. The result would be that you would have more leads, referrals, and information than you would be able to handle.

This is what made John so exceptional at networking—he helped people all the time. He was regularly, proactively, helping a core group of individuals, and they were likewise regularly looking for ways to help him. His approach created numerous mutually beneficial relationships that could be characterized as a core group of people who were working together to help one another. By helping other people, he had created a powerful network! I realized that not only could John do this, but I, or anyone else for that matter, could also implement it. All I needed to do was to focus on helping others succeed! Finally, networking was beginning to make sense as I began focusing on what networking was always intended to be: building relationships.

Networking is not an event

Over the past several years, I have met other introverts who are great at networking. Each one has their own set of tools, but all of them follow the same fundamental rule of helping others first. Sharron was one of those introverts who had learned about networking in an unusual place.

The first time it happened, Sharron was beyond surprised. Another parent on her daughter's swim team called her a couple of weeks after a daylong swim meet. "Sharron, I have been thinking about what you shared with me about how we can make our new project successful."

At the swim meet, Sharron and her new friend had spent over an hour talking about his new project and some of the lessons she had learned from a similar project that she had recently completed. What Sharron didn't know was that her new friend was equally excited to finally be talking to an expert who was more interested in helping his project succeed than in touting her credentials.

"We are looking for someone who really understands our objectives to get this done right. Can you make the time to share your recommendations for our project with our board?" he asked.

Several days later, Sharron met with her new friend and the board. At the meeting, she shared how they could make their project successful and avoid several pitfalls that she had previously encountered. She left the meeting without making a sales pitch, without giving an elevator speech, and without even leaving a brochure behind for them.

The next day they called asking for a proposal. There was no one else they would want to run the project.

When we selflessly help someone else, we are creating the foundation for a relationship. The great thing about networking is that it can happen anywhere that relationships can happen. In Sharron's case, it was at a swim meet. For you, it could be during a project meeting, at church, on the golf course, via email, at an association event, or at a restaurant. The key is that networking is not something that happens exclusively at networking events.

Successful networkers embrace the philosophy that networking isn't an event you attend, but rather a way of living life with a focus on others. The important thing is that you are living your life with the goal of helping others succeed. As you change your philosophy, an amazing thing will begin to happen. Others will work to return the favor. The result is new doors, new opportunities, and new adventures.

To succeed at networking, you still need to embrace association events, trade shows, lunches, etc., as the tools that infuse new relationships into our network. However, don't equate attending an event with Real Networking. Events are where we first learn enough about someone and their business to know how we can help them. Real Networking is the relationship building that occurs after events.

How to help other people

Business relationships are often weakened by years of taking with very little giving in return. To build or strengthen relationships, all you need to do is help the other person without seeking personal gain. The goal is to proactively help make them successful.

Here are some ideas on how you can help someone within your professional network:

1) Refer them to a new client
2) Make an introduction to a potential client
3) Introduce them to a new potential teaming or business partner
4) Send them a useful newspaper article
5) Send them a request for proposal that they might be interested in pursuing
6) Share ideas
7) Share advice

Notice that I didn't tell you to give away your services for free or to otherwise undermine your income ability. I just indicated that you should be helping others that you meet. This is a successful and simple approach that anyone can use, and it yields great success.

Help because you want to, not because you want something

I'll never forget one of the first times I tried to network like an introvert. Over the course of several weeks, I had helped a new friend at least a dozen times and I was anxious to begin seeing the results of my efforts. I decided that it was time to catch up over lunch to see why he wasn't returning the favor.

At lunch, I explained that I had been providing him with multiple leads and information and then asked, "What have you done for me lately?" It was his silence and shock that told me I had completely messed up.

Networking is about relationships, and relationships grow through selfless behavior, not selfish behavior. I had grown to understand the principles that have turned introverts into successful networkers, but I had failed to understand that Real

Networking works only when we are authentic and selfless.

It is amazing how intuitive humans are. I am constantly astonished at how we can see through other's actions and immediately spot selfish behavior. If a sales representative were to call you and ask you about your weekend, you would most likely quickly see through the gesture as a way to soften you up for the sales portion of the call. Just think about how quickly you realized it the first time you received a phone call for a survey that was really just a carefully crafted sales pitch. How many questions were asked until you knew that they were just trying to sell you something?

In the same way, people are very intuitive when it comes to Real Networking. If your goal is to receive a favor in return for your help, you'll quickly undermine your effectiveness. Instead, help others because you want to, not because you want something. For example, if you find yourself thinking about the possible ways someone else can help you, you are probably off track.

Not everyone you help will return the favor. In some cases, you could interact with the same individual for several years and it wouldn't ever occur to them that they should also help you. When I meet someone like this, it is very simple to know how to respond. I simply stop focusing my effort on them. That doesn't mean that I stop helping them altogether, it simply means that they have yet to understand the benefits of networking and, as a result, I choose to direct my efforts toward others.

In the case of my meeting gone wrong, I was thankful for another great human trait; people are forgiving. While I definitely lost some credibility in the short term, my friend and I were able to laugh about it later. We did business together for several years until a job change took him away from my network. Even today, if he called me, I would do anything possible to help him. I truly believe he would do the same for me. That is one of the amazing things about networking like an introvert. When we put others first, they often become true friends that want to help you not because they want something in return, but because they care.

2

THE INTROVERT'S
ADVANTAGE

As I started my new approach, I was feeling better about networking. However, I was still grappling with what it meant to truly network like an introvert. That was when I met Mark. John had opened my eyes to introvert networking, but Mark made me realize that even the most introverted person can be a successful networker.

Mark is one of those people that would be perfectly happy sitting in an enclosed office every day. I met him at an open house hosted by his firm. I can't say we had the easiest of conversations, because we didn't. It wasn't until the next day that I recognized I had met an extreme introvert who was incredible at networking.

In a concisely written follow-up email, Mark introduced me to a new client–a firm I had been unsuccessful meeting until that day. What really tipped me off to what a great networker Mark is was the phone call I received 15 minutes later from the soon-to-be new client.

"Mark sent me a note telling me that we should connect; so I just wanted to see how I can help you," said the voice on the other line.

What had just happened?! Why was it that one

email from Mark would lead to a potential client calling me? The reason, I would soon learn, was the introvert's advantage.

Humans must have relationships to exist. It is an instinct that we are born with, usually nurtured by our parents and explored through adolescence. Over the past two decades, however, we have begun to distort this basic understanding of how humans work. Instead of applying our need for relationships to networking, we have replaced it with sales tactics that, for most people, yield mediocre results. With time, I developed the following networking thesis to better understand this phenomenon:

1. Relationships are the foundation of networking. The exciting news is that this serves as the foundation for why anyone can succeed at building a strong network.

2. Everyone has a God-given instinct to develop relationships. Did you know that everyone on this planet has both a desire and a need to build relationships? My oldest son could be easily classified as an extreme introvert, yet I distinctly remember when he entered preschool how badly he wanted to make friends with others in his class. This same instinct to have friends and relationships applies to everyone, even you.

3. Most people find networking to be difficult. How is it that if networking is all about relationships, and everyone has a God-given instinct to develop relationships, that most people have experienced only failure when networking?

4. The SYSTEM most people think of when they think of "networking" is flawed. Networking is actually much easier than most people think. It isn't the sales tactics that have been taught by networking gurus over the past two decades. It is about building relationships the way we were designed to build relationships.

5. Networking becomes easy if you understand Real Networking. Real Networking is not sales. Instead, it is a focus on building mutually beneficial relationships. Therein lies the true key to succeeding at networking: when you focus on helping others you will gain the rewards of a network that wants to reciprocate by helping you.

It is no wonder that most people feel that networking is difficult or even painful. This is because we have incorrectly defined networking as part of the sales process. We are told to walk into a new group of people armed with brochures and an elevator pitch, two things that were designed to help you sell more effectively, not to help you build relationships more effectively. No doubt this type of "networking" can produce sales, but that is because it is sales. The issue with this sales approach is that the majority of people don't like receiving sales pitches, which can turn them off to the idea of genuine networking.

Just because networking can produce sales doesn't mean that it should be treated as an offshoot of the sales process. This is especially true because everyone has a need for relationships, but not everyone is made to be in sales, just like not everyone was made to be an engineer.

Networking is about building relationships; this is something that, as I noted above, we all have an intrinsic desire to do, anyway. When most people think about networking at an event, they think about "working the room." When an introvert who is applying Real Networking attends an event, they instead focus on helping every person they meet. They make introductions, provide helpful information, and laugh with friends. They focus on relationships instead of themselves.

What I have always found amazing is that Real Networking, that is, building strong relationships based on mutual benefit, is far more successful than showing up to sell everyone your services or products. Instead of "targeting" prospective clients, real networkers are often introduced to prospective clients by mutual friends that they have helped previously. The result is a warm contact that can easily be followed up with over time, enabling the establishment of another networking relationship.

A concentrated approach
– The Introvert's Advantage

While everyone requires relationships, it is fair to say that not everyone requires relationships in the same way. While some extreme extroverts may want to spend every waking hour around others, many introverts would prefer to have far fewer relationships. Some would prefer to have next-to-no relationships. Most of us, of course, fall somewhere in between. The key then is to identify where you fall in the spectrum and to develop relationships that meet your personality type.

For an extreme introvert like Mark, it was easy to develop a highly concentrated approach to relationships. Mark was regularly helping a core group of people that he would probably refer to as friends, including the client he introduced me to. When that client received the email introduction, he wanted to give me a call. I would almost say he was excited to give me a call, because of his trusted friendship with Mark. I later learned that these two friends regularly helped one another and had a network that anyone would covet, one in which several times a week they would help one another through referrals, introductions, and leads.

If you read most books on networking (of which there are many), you will usually see information that is geared toward extroverts: how to work a room, how to effectively meet new people, and what to do at association events. Although these concepts may be fine for a few people, they are not necessarily helpful for most introverts. By embracing who you are as an individual and working with your personal strengths, you can see more success from your network than most extroverts. The secret is to focus on who you are.

Introverts, perhaps without even realizing it, are natural networkers because they have a tendency to focus on a smaller number of relationships. This same concentrated approach can be developed by extroverts, but it is very natural for an introvert to develop a strong core of relationships that can feed them opportunities and information.

One of the keys to networking as an introvert is being yourself. Introverts can excel by developing a strong core group of relationships instead of trying to build a relationship with everyone they meet. The key is to focus on a small, select group of people who are positioned to make you succeed. In an upcoming chapter we will discuss in detail this small group that I refer to as your "Hotlist."

Truly anyone can network

I was in a good friend's office several years ago, discussing how he could better encourage his staff to engage in relationship development with new clients, when he made a comment that stuck with me. Speaking about one of his key employees he said, "He's a great extrovert once he knows you as a friend." How true! I think all of us are a bit like this employee.

In the book "Face to Face," Susan RoAne notes that 93 percent of Americans identify themselves as "shy." If you read into this statistic, it is apparent that the vast majority of extroverts aren't extroverted when it comes to meeting new people. Most of us feel just a bit uncomfortable when we are forced into a situation in which we don't know anyone, and that is why real networking like an introvert is for everyone. It takes the focus off of sales techniques and turns our attention toward real relationship development.

The thing I like most about Real Networking is that anyone can do it. It isn't rocket science, and it certainly does not involve sales techniques. Instead, it focuses on building relationships, and as I said previously, this is something we all need anyway.

3

7 PRINCIPLES OF REAL NETWORKING

I had finally learned what Real Networking was all about. It was not learning a bunch of sales techniques and showing up at a bunch of events that I didn't want to attend. Instead, Real Networking is just about building great relationships. With this knowledge, I began my journey to rewrite the rules of networking as I understood them. What I ended up with through

a series of mishaps, mistakes, and laughter were
the seven principles of real networking.

Principle #1 - Consistency

There isn't anything magical that happens the
first time you meet someone who understands
Real Networking. Most of the time, you'll have a
simple conversation, with hopefully a couple of
laughs about something completely unrelated to
business. You'll walk away with an understanding
of who the person is and how the two of you
could work together. You see, networking isn't
about the first time that you meet; networking is
all about what happens after you meet.

If you and I met, and the following day I helped
you by sending you a lead for a new project that
was perfect for you, you'd probably think I was a
nice guy. If over the following week I helped you
twice more by referring you to two of my clients

that you were interested in working with, you'd probably send me a quick thank-you email. If over the next month I helped you 10 times, with leads, referrals, and information about relevant projects and clients, you'd start taking notice. If over the next two months I helped you in similar capacity 30 times, something amazing would happen. You would begin developing a strong desire to reciprocate the help that you had received. You would want to make certain that I was successful, even as I was focused on making you successful.

What most people miss is that simply helping someone once doesn't get the job done. In the scenario above, the first time I helped you the innate response wasn't to reciprocate; instead, it was simply thinking that I was a nice person. Even after three times, most people will only send a quick thank-you email.

Real Networking happens when we are consistent in applying ourselves to a small group of people called a Hotlist. We'll discuss the Hotlist more in the next chapter, but for now the important thing to note is that you can't consistently help everyone you ever meet. You simply don't have that much time in the day to help even 100 people 30 times per month. Instead, great networkers learn to focus on a core group of people (a Hotlist) so that they can build consistency in their efforts, which is the first principle of networking.

Principle #2 - Be inclusive

Your Hotlist should be small; your network should be broad.

One thing I had to learn the hard way is that not everyone gets it. When I first began to explore what networking really means, I developed a list of people that I was going to help to succeed on a consistent basis. Six months later, I had replaced half of the people on that list for a variety of reasons. One person who stands out in my mind through that process was Rich. He was one of those people who truly appreciated my helping him succeed, and because he had the potential of hiring me directly, he was not only a potential referral source but also a potential client. It wasn't long before he was calling me regularly, asking for information and introductions, even inviting me to his office to train his staff. The only thing he failed to do was to ever help me in return. I think what bothered me most was that I really liked (and still like) Rich; he just didn't get it.

During this same time, I was trying out something else to see how it worked. It worked so well that it became the second principle of networking.

Instead of focusing exclusively on my Hotlist, I began to be inclusive and help everyone I could.

Now, I knew I couldn't help everyone 10 times per month, but I was fairly confident that I could help most people I met at least once. So I began helping everyone every day. It was a simple philosophy that was probably a bit altruistic, but the results were astounding. As I helped others, I noticed that my effort opened new doors to new opportunities. It established new relationships where none had previously existed. Most importantly, it established my reputation as someone who was just interested in helping others succeed. In less than half a year, my relationships were growing and changing in new ways that I never could have anticipated.

As those relationships grew, so did my frustration with Rich. I knew that he could help me, so I began trying to find out what I was doing wrong that kept him from reciprocating. After months of searching, I finally figured it out…not everyone gets it.

I was faced with a dilemma: what should I do with my one-way friendship with Rich? Every ounce of me wanted to drop him like a ton of bricks from a tall skyscraper, but I knew inside that wasn't the right answer. That was when I realized that principle #2 was important to successful networking. By being inclusive and helping everyone I meet, it became easy for me to graciously release Rich from my Hotlist and continue to help him when I had time. It was also easy because through my efforts in reaching out to others I had meet Ken; a true friend who I knew would fill the void in my network.

What I learned is that helping everyone every day isn't just a noble perspective on life; instead, it is a valuable approach that will help you to reach your long-term goals. And the best part is that you will get to reach those goals surrounded by friends and people who also want you to succeed.

Principle #3 - Be genuine

"What have you done for me lately?" I had just begun to figure out what Real Networking was all about and, if my friend's facial expression was any indication, I still had a lot to learn. In the first chapter I shared with you briefly about the major mistake I made when I sat down with Ted and asked him this "relationship undermining" question. What unfolded, however, was much bigger than that. Ted was a great guy who worked in the same industry I did, so it didn't take me very long to add him to my initial Hotlist.

Over the eight weeks leading up to our conversation, I had tried diligently to help Ted in any way that I could. The good news was that because we served similar client types, I had already been able to help him. I referred him to ten of my clients that needed his services. The bad news was that my inept networking ability had just shone through as I sat across the lunch table asking him what he had done for me. It didn't take a psychologist to see that my comment had just undermined a growing relationship.

Most people have a handful of gauges that they use when they meet someone new. One gauge that people use tells them if the person they are talking to is being genuine or just trying to get something out of them. Several years ago, I had a siding contractor come to our home to give us a quote on some new siding. As the young man walked into our house, he quickly began talking about our dogs, kids, and photographs around the house. It didn't take long to realize that he was just trying to connect with us on a personal level in an effort to increase his chances of selling us siding. We all have this "genuine" meter that tells us when someone is being a friend because they like us or if it is because they want something. In the case with Ted, I had just learned the third principle of networking: when you help someone, you need to do it because you truly want to help them, not because you want something in return. What I didn't expect to learn during that same meeting with Ted was the fourth principle of networking: Make certain you are heard.

Principle #4 - Make certain you are heard

After I posed my question to Ted, I could see he had absolutely no clue what I was talking about. So I began to clarify my statement by recounting each of the clients and projects that I had referred to him. I was shocked to find out that, out of the ten, only six had ever called him. To make matters worse, only one of those six had mentioned my name. It turned out that my friend wasn't failing me; instead, I failed to ensure he knew that I was helping him.

It is not difficult to ensure that you are being heard. Today when I make a referral, I usually email the contact information of the person I am referring, instead of just giving it over the phone. Simple enough, but the following steps ensure that my contact knows about the referral.

As soon as the referral is sent, I forward a copy of the email to the person I just referred. Now I have helped them to know the referral is coming, and I have ensured that they know I gave them a referral to begin with. Even if the person never reaches out to them, they will know that I am working to help them. I refer to this as "making certain you are heard." Regardless of what happens with the referral, I can be confident that my friends know I was thinking about them and trying to help them be successful.

Principle #5 - Say "Thank You"

If you were to open my top left desk drawer, you would find two things in it, a bottle of wine and a bottle of champagne. Those two thank-you gifts have led to some of the largest contracts I have ever had the opportunity to bring in, a result that I believe is firmly rooted in the fact that we live in an overtly underappreciated society.

When speaking on the topic of networking, I often ask how many people in the room have received a thank-you note in the past three months, and the answer is almost always less than 5% of the group. The only exception is when I ask the question just after Christmas, when about 40% of the room will indicate that they have received a thank-you note. What that means is if you take the time to thank people, your gratitude will make you stand out from the crowd.

It is my practice to send a bottle of wine to say thanks when I am referred to a new client and the referral turns into a new project. In a similar light, I send a bottle of champagne when I land a new contract from someone with whom I have been networking. While using gifts, how you say thank you should be as individual and as unique as you are. I know many people who will take others out to lunch, send thank-you cards, or even give a gift certificate. It doesn't really matter how you do it. The most important point is that you do it.

Principle #6 - Make certain your contact gets the credit

After several years of networking I was enjoying watching my relationships change and grow.

Instead of simply connecting with my peers, I was beginning to build relationships with the upper-level management in many notable companies. It was an energizing turn of events that I had not expected, and one that I was unfortunately not prepared to handle.

I was truly excited. It is fairly easy to refer a new client to a friend, and often it is even easier to make an introduction, but this was one of those rare opportunities in which I was able to ensure that a friend on my Hotlist received a new project. You might think that I am a little crazy for being excited about landing a contract for someone else, but that is what Real Networking is all about; a sense of friendship and camaraderie that celebrates each other's success.

As I was picking up the phone, a thought occurred to me. What if I called the company's CEO instead? He and I had met several times and he was becoming a friend, and I knew this contract would be a good way to strengthen our relationship. So, abandoning two years of relationship building through networking, I called him instead of my contact. It was a good conversation, but I could immediately see that he was not nearly as enthusiastic as my contact would have been. Instead, it was as if I was just starting over in building the consistency principle we looked at first. Worse was that I took away any chance for my true friend to look great in front of the CEO of the company. I had undermined his efforts by going over him when it really counted.

I decided then and there that the only way to ensure success when networking was to make certain that my contacts received the credit, not me. What is amazing about this philosophy is that, by ensuring that they receive the credit, it almost always comes around as they provide you with the recognition publicly. That's a much better position to be in than to simply tout your own successes.

Principle #7 – Remember the snowball theory of networking

I distinctly remember two things I enjoyed every winter during my childhood: sledding and watching Looney Tunes. In those old cartoons, there was always an episode in which someone would start a snowball rolling at the top of a hill. By the time it reached the bottom it would grow into a mammoth ball of snow. Of course, some unsuspecting character would inevitably get embedded into the snowball as it rolled over them and it would subsequently smash into an inanimate object near the bottom of the hill. So, as a youngling, I sought to replicate the experiment.

I vividly remember sitting at the top of a sled hill in Morgantown, West Virginia, packing the perfect starter ball, and of course one of my unsuspecting older brothers was at the bottom of the hill. As I gave it a little push I was a bit disappointed to see that it only rolled a couple of inches before coming to a stop. So I began to modify my approach by building the snowball a little bigger before I gave it its next push down the hill. Sure enough, a little bit more and the added weight carried it a little further. After several attempts, I had it! With a bit of up-front work, I could make a snowball big enough to grow on its own as it rolled all the way down the hill, although I never could get it large enough to squash one of my brothers.

Networking works the same way. It takes effort and determination to build Real Networking relationships, but the result is incredible. As you grow your network, you will begin to build momentum without additional effort. I am regularly amazed at how my network has taken me to places that I never anticipated going as new doors and opportunities have opened before me. It isn't that I am doing something special; it is just that there is power in relationships. As you build your network, you'll find that the same is true for you.

4

DEVELOPING A HOTLIST

I don't remember exactly when it happened, but I distinctly remember the feeling I had when I realized that I wasn't the only person with whom John had developed a mutually beneficial relationship. John had somewhere between 10 and 20 close professional relationships (I would later begin to refer to this core group of friends as a Hotlist). In my mind, I multiplied the number of leads, referrals, introductions, and help that I was giving John by the number of friends in his Hotlist, and then I froze. John was a genius; a genius with a seemingly unending supply of new opportunities.

Set up a plan to succeed and focus on a core group of people

Once I learned the secret to networking, I jumped right into helping those I met. It didn't take long to recognize that not everyone I was helping was returning the favor. As I looked at the situation more, I began to realize that many of the people I was networking with were not inside my same "circle of influence," as Stephen R. Covey describes it in "The 7 Habits of Highly Effective People."

It wasn't that they were unwilling to help, it was because of what they did for a living or because of the company that they worked for—they simply were not in a position to reciprocate. It became clear that I needed to refine my network. In addition, I was helping so many people that my efforts weren't building a strong sense of urgency for others to reciprocate. It seemed that the large group of people I was helping was beginning to dilute my effectiveness.

Based on this discovery, I began the process of weaning the individuals who were not able to reciprocate my help and instead focused my attention on relationships that were more central to my industry and work. I found that the people I could help the most and those that could help me the most were not clients, but peers who provided complementary services to the same clients I served. In fact, I realized that finding people to network with was the easy part, but finding the right people in my same circle of influence was more difficult.

The good news for you is that you get to skip that part. Instead of weaning people from a long list, you can start right now by selecting the right individuals for your Hotlist. Remember, the great thing about Real Networking is that it creates mutually beneficial relationships in which two people are consistently looking for ways to help one another. The key to this happening is concentrated effort on a specific group of people that over time develops into multiple, mutually beneficial relationships.

Why only focus on a small group of people? Because networking succeeds when it creates a sense of urgency to reciprocate between two people. In Principle #1 found in the previous chapter, we looked at the importance of consistency, and I gave the example of helping you by providing you with one lead or referral and how you would feel grateful. In the same example, when I provided you with ten leads and ten referrals a month, or 30 in two months, you developed a healthy desire to help me, even proactively looking for opportunities to return the favor. This focus on an individual builds a strong sense of urgency as both people work to help one another. The urgency that is developed by helping someone will keep you in the forefront of their mind, and them in the forefront of your mind. As a result, both parties benefit as the relationship develops and you are actively motivated to help one another.

To start networking you just need to take two first steps: 1) recognize that networking is nothing less than helping other people without expecting anything in return, and 2) try out your new networking skills on a core group of people that I'll refer to as your Hotlist.

Generating a Hotlist

Your Hotlist should be a group of 10 to 20 people who are in your same circle of influence. An easy way to generate your Hotlist is to start by thinking about the relationships that you need in order to succeed. These relationships may include others in your industry, your circle of influence, or even your company if you work for a large multifaceted business. Take a moment to write down the top 10 people you need to succeed and rate the strength of those relationships.

How you are doing? Are these relationships weak or strong? Are they just names linked to job titles, or are they people with whom you have an investment in mutual interests? Most people will find a mixed bag: some relationships that are incredibly strong and others that are just names on a list. These key relationships will serve as a basis for the establishment of your Hotlist.

Requirements for a Hotlist:
- People who provide complementary services to your same clients
- People who are in your same circle of influence
- People who represent a cross section of your industry
- People you can help
- People who are in a position to help you

Once you have identified this group of key relationships, expand the list by writing down the names of people you work with on a regular basis. These should not simply be clients, but rather individuals that you work with from a variety of areas. Consider people from every aspect of your career, including:

- Project managers
- Consultants
- Clients
- Sub-consultants
- Support staff

As you write your list, glance through your Outlook contacts list or other database. You'll be amazed at how many people you interacted with in the past year. I recall the first time I did this exercise. I was surprised to see that I had connected, at least superficially, with several hundred people in the previous 12 months.

Once you have generated your list, begin identifying the handful of people on the list with whom you really connect. Strong networks have individuals not simply from one area of business, but rather from a cross section of areas. Try to choose only one or two individuals that perform the same services. For example, you should only have one or two attorneys on your list. Look for friends you enjoy working with and perhaps whom you have helped previously or who have helped you previously. Don't worry about making the wrong choices at this stage; many of the people you select now will be filtered on and off of your list over the next couple of months as you work to refine it.

Your Hotlist should be people that are in your same circle of influence, people that represent a cross section of your industry, people who are in a position to help you, and people you can help.

Once you have a Hotlist, do something about it!

After I met John, I knew I needed to start implementing a new approach to networking. It was easy to decide to start networking, but I didn't quite know where to start.

As I was reading the paper the next day, I ran across an informative article and decided to send it to a couple of friends in the industry. They were just a couple of people that I had been working with on previous projects, and some people I should have been following-up with anyway. To my surprise, all of them replied within minutes with a simple "thanks." One of them wrote a longer note about how he had just been looking for that information. I had my answer. Focusing on helping others didn't mean that I suddenly had to go to a networking event and try to pick off potential clients. I just needed to start with my current circle of friends and look for opportunities to help them.

Remember, the best way to build a relationship is simply to help other people; not because you want something, but simply because you want to build the relationship. Business relationships are often weakened by years of taking with very little giving in return. To strengthen a relationship, all you need to do is help the other person without seeking personal gain. The goal is to proactively work to make their life easier and more productive.

Take your Hotlist to the next level

Every time I was in John's office, it seemed that the phone would ring or an email would come through from someone in his network. It got to the point that some days I thought John had to know everyone in the industry. It was as if he had a system in place to develop relationships in such a way that everyone would know him long before they ever even spoke with him.

Because John was so well known, it was easy for him to connect with almost anyone. But as I sat in his office, I was surprised to realize that he wasn't the person making the calls. Other people were always connecting with him. I was excited that my small network of friends was already providing me with leads and making my life easier, but I likewise wanted to get to a point where others in the industry were reaching out and initiating the relationship development process. It was time to expand my network.

The key to building the size of your network is the same one you use to build your relationships with the individuals on your Hotlist. You start by helping other people. Although this is a simple concept, it can be difficult to implement because it requires a change in how you approach life—it requires a paradigm shift. It is relatively easy to engage a small group of people, such as your Hotlist, and focus on helping them succeed. It is measurable and, as such, the results can be evaluated. What I saw, and what you will see in relatively short order, is that Real Networking works.

The paradigm shift is a lifestyle change that focuses on helping everyone you come into contact with every day. It redefines the value you place on others compared to yourself.

As every parent can attest, children are inherently self-focused, and you were no exception (if you disagree, a call to your parents may be able to clarify this for you).

To build your network and reputation, you must defy this standard and be willing to help others first. I'm not talking about putting everyone else in the world ahead of yourself; rather, I'm talking about helping others in the same way that you would like others to help you. It is "loving your neighbor as yourself," to quote probably the most famous relationship guru of all time. Because this does not come naturally to most of us, we need to change how we think about people and how we interact with them. We need to be intentional in our relationships.

Real Networking isn't a set of formulas and tools. It is a fresh approach to life, and you have the opportunity to change your perspective. Over the years, I have begun the transformation of working to help everyone I meet. I can't say that I am always successful, but I can tell you that the rewards are bountiful. Some people I help may never have stopped to say "thank you" on their path to reach a goal, but others have become some of my best friends.

Over time, your Hotlist will change. You will find that not everyone you picked to start your Hotlist understands Real Networking. Some of them, however, may become the business partners that are the foundation for your greatest successes. As people fall off your original hot list, you will find others who truly understand networking, and your life will become full of relationships that truly matter.

The great thing about Real Networking is that regardless of your successes and failures, you will be living a life that is seeking the best interests of others and helping them to achieve their goals. The fruit is friendship and a fresh perspective on business and life. For me, the choice was simple, and I hope that it is equally simple for you.

5

SETTING A PLAN

I am often asked the following question during training sessions on Networking, "Why should I network?" It is a simple question that has an answer which can change the way you interact with others and the way you live your life. The powerful truth of why you should network is that Real Networking is about you and others, not about a company, although your company will benefit from your networking.

If you are a project manager, the projects you work on will stay at your company when you leave. If you are an engineer, the designs you work on will stay at your company when you leave. If you are an accountant, the money you work with had better stay at your company when you leave. One of the few things that you will take with you (and that your company will lose) is your relationships, also known as your network. Because of this, your network is one of your most powerful tools for your career and life. Let's look at two extremes of how networking plays a role in careers.

Top performer vs. relationships

An executive in the midst of an economic downturn was faced with a problem. He had to lay off one of two people. The first was an incredible performer with a knack for completing projects on time and without errors. He also never seemed to bring new work in the door. The second was a good performer with a network of relationships that was bringing several million dollars of work into the company each year. Who was laid off? Time and time again, we see that most executives will protect the welfare of the company by keeping a good performer who can bring work in the door over an incredible performer who isn't bringing in work.

Strong networkers are spared during layoffs, not because they are top performers in job-related tasks, but because they have something that many top performers don't have. Their network helps them to secure a long-term future for themselves and for their company.

A promoted career

Your network not only protects you, it also reminds management to ensure that you stay around for a long time. Because of this, top networkers are also regularly the first promoted. Take the story of Mark, a non-engineer who works at a top engineering firm in Washington, D.C. After he joined the firm, it didn't take long for the owners to recognize that they had found someone who knew how to bring work in the door. In just a few short years, Mark was promoted to partner ahead of many registered engineers that were his senior. It was during the recession that followed, however, that everyone learned just how key that promotion was. Mark navigated his branch office through the difficult time and continued to bring new work in the door, even as competitors in the region were closing offices.

If you want to advance your career, do everything in your power to bring work, solutions, and answers to your company. The most effective way to do this is through Real Networking, which involves continually helping others and building a close group of friends to whom you purposefully focus your help. I know that my company would survive without me, but I have satisfaction in doing everything in my power to make our company succeed. When you live your life to help others, you are learning how to build a successful life!

Your next steps

You're ready to start, you've thought through your options, and the choice is clear: Real Networking is for you. The key is to act now. The following sections will walk you through the steps to start your network.

Write down your Hotlist

We already discussed the importance of your Hotlist in Chapter 4. Therefore, begin right now by putting pen to paper and writing down the names of at least 10 individuals that meet the requirements of someone in your Hotlist. These are individuals that should be in your primary circle of influence, people representing a cross section of your industry, people who are in a position to help you, and people you can help.

Writing down your Hotlist serves two functions. First, it makes the list measurable, and second, it makes it memorable. Measurable because you can track how effectively you are reaching out to the group, and memorable because writing it down will ensure you remember whom you are targeting.

As you begin to leverage your Hotlist by intentionally helping those listed, you'll find yourself wanting to identify those individuals who understand the concept of reciprocity in the relationship. Remember that 50% of the people on my first Hotlist were replaced within the first six months, so don't be surprised if the same thing happens to you.

Memorable is important because you will want to make certain you help everyone on your Hotlist at least twice a month. Writing the list down will help you to identify who on your list you need to follow up with.

Set up triggers and reminders

Writing down your Hotlist is easy; remembering to follow up with everyone three months from now is hard. In order to make certain I continue to focus on networking, I have developed a number of easy reminders and triggers to ensure that I am regularly building my network relationships.

Reminders: The first thing I did was to add everyone in my Hotlist to Microsoft Outlook. I then set a "flag" reminder for each of them for two weeks out. Then, each time I help someone in my Hotlist, I simply re-flag them two weeks out again. By doing this I always receive a reminder if I haven't helped someone in my Hotlist in the past two weeks. This same approach can be taken with most every CRM (Client Relationship Management) program that you may already be using. The software isn't important; only the reminder to follow up is important.

Triggers: The second thing I did was to set up weekly "triggers" to remind me to help others. Triggers are things that I am already doing that I can dual-purpose to help others. Let me give you an example. For the past decade, I read the *Washington Business Journal* each week. It was a very easy transition for me to also think about my Hotlist when I read news articles and forward articles that I knew would be helpful to specific people on my Hotlist.

This has become especially easy in recent years, as I have been able to read the newspaper online or on a tablet and digitally forward articles. The idea wasn't to add a brand-new activity that would take me extra time each week, but instead to dual-purpose an activity that I was already doing to help others.

Some other examples include dual-purposing networking events to help others in my Hotlist meet key contacts; dual-purposing webinars I planned on attending and paying for anyway by inviting others to watch them in our conference room with me; dual-purposing weekly in-house meetings to support others' ideas at my company; and dual-purposing client project meetings to talk in front of our client about what others in my Hotlist had done right. In each of these cases, your goal is to multiply your effectiveness by helping others without adding new activities.

Start asking the right question

The fundamental networking question we looked at in the beginning of this book is, "What can I do to help this person?" When you meet new people and see existing colleagues, start each conversation by asking yourself what you can do to help them. This is especially easy when you simply start with the people you have contact with every day, such as clients, project managers, and colleagues.

Get Involved!

Real Networking is about taking action, so the worst thing that you can do after reading this book is nothing at all. Probably the easiest way that you can start is by becoming involved in associations where your clients and others inside your same circle of influence hang out.

For years I have been a member of the Society for Marketing Professional Services, because almost every firm in my industry is represented there: clients and complementary services firms. This unique mix of people has been one of the keys to building a great network. Because my clients are not "targets" when I am networking, it is easy to build meaningful relationships with them without them feeling like I am just another salesperson.

When you start working on a new project with a new team, something interesting usually happens. The first meeting is all business, talking about the project itself and how to meet the goals as a team. But did you ever notice that after a couple of meetings, more personal things start to be discussed? People start talking about their interests, their families, and the fun things they did last weekend. It is seemingly painless to foster and build relationships when you are working together.

Most people overlook the fact that professional or community associations can work the same way for them. When you get involved in an association, you'll often find that you are able to build relationships easily because people are meeting around common interests. I know dozens of introverts that have used this model to painlessly build relationships in their industry. The results are almost universally the same – they actually look forward to going to association events! Why? They feel as if they are heading out to laugh and talk with friends, not to try to be a salesperson. When you get involved, you'll find that others start to reach out to you. Intentionally involving yourself with groups of people ends up being the catalyst to building new relationships.

This same principle can be applied to nontraditional activities. I know one engineer who liked to play golf, so he worked with his marketing department to start a summer golf group for the industry. Today, he is well known and enjoys a continual stream of new relationships from people that want to meet him to join the group.

Network Like an Introvert

It is often easy to see when something you are doing isn't working but difficult to make the changes needed to succeed. I personally spent years learning the wrong way to network, focused on myself and my goals. It was when I finally decided to throw out what I had been taught and start over that networking finally started working for me.

I learned that networking is about relationships, and that relationships grow when we focus on helping other people instead of helping ourselves. I learned that Real Networking is built on seven principles that shape our actions and our relationships. I learned to focus on a Hotlist, a core group of people that I can foster into mutually beneficial relationships. And I learned that Real Networking is a change in how you approach other people; not just 10 or 20 people, but everyone that you meet.

I hope that you will choose to make the same decision: that you will also choose to learn how to network like an introvert. Start where you are today, be consistent, and enjoy seeing where it takes you. I have no doubt that your life will change in unexpected and exciting ways, just as mine has.

ABOUT THE AUTHOR

Tim Klabunde is a Fellow from Johns Hopkins University and the founder of the Design and Construction Network. He is a recognized expert on the intersection of relationships and marketing. His track record includes work for notable public companies, in addition to some of the largest private design and construction firms in the country. An avid writer and speaker, Tim has been published and quoted in numerous publications including: the Washington Business Journal, CE News, Marketer, Commonwealth Contractor, MarketingNow, Business Owner Magazine, A/E Rainmaker, and the Design & Construction Report.